Royal River

A GUIDE TO THE RIVER THAMES

FRONT COVER: *The bascules of Tower Bridge are raised to allow a Thames sailing barge to pass through.*

ABOVE: *A pleasure launch sails by Windsor Castle, whose Round Tower dominates the scene.*

BACK COVER: *The Thames Barrier consists of a series of movable gates built side-by-side across the river.*

ROYAL RIVER

Michael St John Parker

Measured by the standards of the Amazon or the Nile, the Yangtze or the Danube, the Thames is a provincial stream of almost insignificant size; yet its history and its role in the life of the English nation entitle it to a place among the great rivers of the world, and it exerts a peculiar magic and power of its own, which have caused it to be a source of fascination and delight to countless generations.

For centuries it has carried the traffic and served the trade of one of the greatest merchant cities known to history; it has seen savage battles and mighty pageants, has flowed indifferently past the wildest extremes of wealth and poverty, has been both a pestilential open sewer and the inspiration of poets and painters.

London itself owes its origin and much of its wealth to the influence of the river, as the latest archaeological discoveries of wharfs and other relics of Roman and medieval times make clear. It is true that the great ships no

longer come to the Pool of London, and the landward growth of the city has diminished the relative importance of its old watery highway; but still the best way to see London from its natural centre is to travel by boat along the Thames, and today, thanks to the cleansing and restoration work of the last 30 years, it is possible to enjoy the experience more, perhaps, than at any time in the last two centuries.

Whatever changes it may have seen and undergone, in one respect the Thames remains as it has been since the time of Alfred the Great – it is a royal river, strung with palaces like precious stones on a necklace and rich in majestic associations. To take a boat along the Thames is to follow in the wake of countless royal journeys, and where better to begin our voyage than at Windsor, beneath the frowning walls and lofty towers of one of the oldest and grandest of all the royal castles.

William the Conqueror first established a fortress here, on a bluff above the river plain, and nearly every monarch since then has added his or her contribution to make the castle stronger, or more splendid, or just more habitable. It is still a fortress, as guards in scarlet tunics and beetling bearskins bear imperturbable witness – and a shrine of medieval chivalry, too, with the chapel of the Order of the Garter in the outer ward. But it is also the principal seat of the Royal House of Windsor, to which, indeed, it has given its name.

The outline plan of the courtyards has not altered much since the 12th century, but the buildings themselves have been remodelled to meet the changing requirements of the royal family who, since George III, have taken a particular delight in Windsor Castle, favouring it as a private as well as a public residence. Much work was done in the early 19th

century by Sir Jeffry Wyatville, architect to George IV, who restored walls and towers dismantled in the time of Charles II, raised the Round Tower to its present commanding height, and remodelled the magnificent, treasure-crammed State Apartments. Queen Victoria, in her turn, spent money lavishly on Windsor, and the Castle is steeped in associations with the Queen-Empress, who lies buried with her husband, Prince Albert, in Frogmore Mausoleum in the Home Park.

Many kings have hunted in these parklands (and not only kings, it seems, for it is said that the Great Park is haunted by the sinister, stag-headed apparition of Herne the Hunter, with his deadly hounds!). George III established a model farm here, and modern monarchs enjoy the pleasures of racing at Ascot in one of the most colourful weeks of the English social season.

Just across the river from Windsor, and so close by that from certain view-points its battlemented halls and turrets merge with the castle's mightier towers, is another royal foundation of legendary splendour – Eton College, the charity school that became the nursery of a ruling class. Five patrician centuries have endowed it with a uniquely rich and brilliant history, so that its very stones seem to speak of prime ministers and poets, generals and judges, the rich, the brilliant and the powerful, who have spent their schooldays there – often, until the present century, in conditions of extraordinary squalor and brutality! It is a curiously open place, however, in feeling at least; some schools turn their backs monastically on the world, others confront it with severe and threatening disapproval, but Eton waits with serene assurance for the world to come a-courting.

FACING PAGE: *Rowing has long been a popular sport at Eton College. The cox of the senior boat is seen here, wearing admiral's uniform, together with the Captain of Boats and another oarsman. They are dressed for the Fourth of June festival, which celebrates George III's birthday; he was closely connected with the school.*

ABOVE: *Eton College from the east bank of the Thames. This view is described in Thomas Gray's famous 'Ode on a Distant Prospect of Eton College':*

Ye distant spires, ye antique
    towers,
That crown the wat'ry glade,
Where grateful Science still adores
Her Henry's holy Shade;
And ye, that from the stately brow
Of Windsor's heights th' expanse
    below
Of grove, of lawn, of mead survey,
Whose turf, whose shade, whose
    flowers among
Wanders the hoary Thames along
His silver-winding way.

RIGHT: *Feeding the swans and ducks on an autumn day at Windsor.*

The royal splendours of Eton and Windsor are aptly balanced, at least for those with a sense of irony, by the site at Runnymede, a little way downstream, of one of the English Crown's most notable reverses. Here, on 15 June, 1215, King John was forced to concede to his rebellious barons a long list of privileges – the Great Charter, which, improbably enough, later came to be regarded as the foundation stone of British constitutional liberties.

Rights of a different kind are

*

FACING PAGE, ABOVE: *Hampton Court Palace. In the foreground is the colourful array of the Pond Garden, which was originally laid out c. 1700 and remodelled earlier this century.*

FACING PAGE, BELOW: *Aerial view of Hampton Court Palace, clearly showing the West Front with its Great Gatehouse dating from Henry VIII's time. Stretching eastwards beyond the Great Fountain is the Long Water.*

ABOVE: *A tranquil scene at Hampton, where sailing is a favourite pastime.*

marked by the London Stone at Staines, the next town along the river. Here in 1285 was set the upper limit of the authority wielded by the medieval port of London – an indication of the wealth already enjoyed at that time by the city merchants.

Chertsey, Shepperton (of film studios fame) and Molesey bring us to the next of the great palaces which line the banks of the lower Thames: Hampton Court, often regarded as the richest, and certainly the largest of English royal residences. It was first built by Cardinal Wolsey, whose power and pride were stunningly demonstrated by its thousand rooms, large and small, with their sumptuous decorations. Such opulence attracted the envy and eventually the distrust of the king, Henry VIII, and Wolsey felt obliged to present his palace to the Crown in 1525. The royal extortioner spent more than one of his honeymoons there; the future Edward VI was born there at the cost of his mother's life; and there Catherine Howard was arrested – her ghost is said to haunt the Long Gallery, still screaming for mercy.

William III, 150 years after these

Tudor melodramas were played, commissioned Sir Christopher Wren to carry out an extensive remodelling of the palace. The resulting State Apartments and gardens, together with the spreading grounds themselves – a remarkable survival of late 17th-century landscape gardening – stand among Wren's greatest achievements. Their staid, almost homely dignity can be set in sharp, fascinating contrast with the coldly absolutist arrogance of Louis XIV's Versailles, which was being built at the same time.

No monarch has lived at Hampton Court since George II. George III is said to have conceived a dislike for the place when a boy, as a result of having his ears publicly boxed by his grandfather one day in the State Apartments. For generations now the palace, with its priceless treasures, has been open to the public as part of the national heritage.

Beyond Hampton Court the river curves northwards to Kingston-on-Thames, a borough which, as its name suggests, boasts ancient associations with royalty. It was the favoured

coronation place of 10th-century Saxon kings, and their Coronation Stone is still preserved outside the Guildhall.

At Teddington Lock, below Kingston, the Thames becomes a tidal stream, and from this point the river is controlled by the Port of London Authority whose limits stretch down as far as the Tongue Lightship (opposite Margate). The sights crowd thicker and thicker. Richmond and Twickenham, on opposite banks of the river, were much patronised by leaders of society from the late 17th century onwards – the politicians, the wits, the bright stars of fashion. Some of their houses still remain: Ham House, on the Richmond side, retains remarkable examples of Stuart decor and furnishings, while opposite in Twickenham is the Orleans House Gallery, built by James Gibbs in 1720, and the Palladian elegance of Marble Hill House, created for a mistress of George II. Alexander Pope lived at Twickenham, and a relic of his

elaborate gardens remains in the form of a mutilated but still curious 'grotto'. A much more important, and complete, survival of 18th-century dilettantism is Horace Walpole's fantasy house, Strawberry Hill, also at Twickenham; here, some would say, is the fountain-head of the movement known as the Gothic Revival.

More varied – and vulgar – associations cluster round Eel-Pie Island; Henry VIII stopped his barge there to enjoy the delicacy which gave the place its name, wealthy Edwardians threw notoriously extravagant parties in the hotel there, and the Rolling Stones performed in a 1960's nightclub. But on the firmer ground of the river banks we are back with royal palaces and stately memories.

Richmond is a royal manor of almost immemorial antiquity, and the palace which once stood there was a favourite residence of Plantagenet and Tudor rulers. Edward III died here, and so, amid deathbed drama and intrigue, did

Elizabeth I. In lighter vein, the charming traditional air 'On Richmond Hill' still carries echoes of the philandering pursuits of the Prince Regent in the early years of the 19th century, when the view from Richmond Hill seems, if we can trust the painted record, to have been as idyllic as any in England. White Lodge in Richmond Park, now occupied by the Royal Ballet School, saw the birth of the future King Edward VIII in 1894.

Isleworth, on the north bank, still boasts some fine 17th- and 18th-century mansions, and a pillared boathouse attributed to the landscape architect Capability Brown; but this stretch of the river is dominated by the ducal grandeurs of Syon House, London residence of the Percys, dukes of Northumberland, who made it a centre for political plots and intrigues in Tudor and Stuart times. The house was reshaped in palatial style from 1762 onwards by Robert Adam, and the grounds (which now contain a garden

FACING PAGE: *The river near Teddington Lock.*

TOP: *Marble Hill House with its beautifully laid out grounds.*

RIGHT: *Ham House, built in 1610. It now contains treasures from the Victoria and Albert Museum.*

ABOVE: *The Thames at Richmond is a popular subject with local artists.*

centre) were laid out by Capability Brown.

Practically opposite Syon Park are the Royal Botanic Gardens at Kew, a world-famous centre of scientific botany. Its 300 acres of gardens form one of the most beautiful pleasure-grounds in all England, especially when daffodils, bluebells or rhododendrons are in bloom. Some 45,000 species of plants grow in the gardens, and over 7,000,000 dried specimens are preserved in the Herbarium. The gardens were founded in 1759 by Princess Augusta, mother of George III; it was at her behest that Sir William Chambers built the delightful, 163 feet high Chinese Pagoda. George III was particularly fond of the charming 17th-century, Dutch-style house known as Kew Palace, and many souvenirs of this much-misunderstood monarch are to be found there.

From Kew to Chiswick Mall past Strand-on-the-Green the waterfronts are adorned by elegant houses. Pride of them all is Chiswick House, an exquisite Palladian villa begun in 1725 to the designs of the connoisseur Lord Burlington, assisted by William Kent; both men lie buried in St Nicholas' church nearby. It is perhaps one of the most aristocratic buildings ever erected in England, and its quality has survived even the attentions of modern government ministries. For a century after its completion the rich, the clever

Continued on page 12

★

FACING PAGE, ABOVE: *The 18th-century pub, the London Apprentice, Isleworth, reputedly an old smugglers' haunt.*

FACING PAGE, BELOW: *Syon House. The interior demonstrates some of the finest examples of Robert Adam's work.*

ABOVE RIGHT: *The well-loved view of the Thames from Richmond Hill.*

RIGHT: *White Lodge, now the home of the Royal Ballet School, was built in 1729 for George II.*

FACING PAGE, ABOVE LEFT: *Kew Palace, originally built in 1631 for a London merchant.*

FACING PAGE, ABOVE RIGHT: *The Japanese Gateway in Kew Gardens.* FACING PAGE, BELOW: *The elegant,* Italian-inspired Chiswick House. ABOVE: *Some pretty riverside dwellings at Strand-on-the-Green.*

and the powerful thronged here, but it was perhaps always more a showcase than a home.

Nowadays this stretch of the river is more famous for oarsmen than for aristocrats; Mortlake and Hammersmith, Barnes and Putney, are names made famous by Oxford and Cambridge Boat Race commentaries, and the boathouses of London rowing-clubs line the south bank towards Fulham.

Fulham itself is an ugly district adorned by a famous and popular football club; Hurlingham House, now an exclusive club and formerly a famous polo club; and Fulham Palace, the venerable residence of the bishops of London, with 1200 years of un-interrupted ecclesiastical history.

The south bank of the river from this point onwards is grimly and determinedly industrial. The most striking landmark of the reach is Battersea power-station: at the time of its building, in the 1930s, it was seen as a triumph of progress, a monument to the idealism of 'modern planning'; now it is no longer operational, but there are plans to turn it into a leisure centre. The Victorian cast-iron elegance of Albert Bridge, on the other hand, wears well, and the vista of this happily ornamental structure, fes-tive with lights and colour, cheers the mind like champagne.

Chelsea, on the north bank,

*

ABOVE LEFT: *Fulham Palace, part of which dates from the 16th century.*

LEFT: *The Oxford and Cambridge Boat Race has been an annual event on the Thames since 1856. The crews row from Putney to Mortlake.*

FACING PAGE, ABOVE: *Hammersmith Bridge, originally built in 1827, was partly demolished and rebuilt by Sir Joseph Bazelgette. The current bridge, retaining the original stone-work, was completed in 1887.*

FACING PAGE, BELOW: *The pub called The Dove was supposedly a favourite meeting place of Charles II and Nell Gwynne.*

offers a fascinating contrast to Battersea. From the 16th century, when Sir Thomas More had a mansion by the riverside here, Chelsea has combined the character of a fashionable suburb with that of an intellectual and artistic Latin quarter; its style and verve make it one of the most distinctive of London's 'villages'. Fielding, Smollett, Turner, Mrs Gaskell, Carlyle, George Eliot, Rossetti, Swinburne, Whistler, Oscar Wilde, Sargent, Wilson Steer, Augustus John, Lloyd George are only some of the famous names associated with Chelsea. Several of these people lived in the row of waterfront houses known as Cheyne Walk.

Easily the most distinguished building to be seen along the Chelsea Embankment is the Royal Hospital, founded by Charles II in 1682 for the support of army veterans, and designed by Sir Christopher Wren. Its three splendid quadrangles, parts of which are open to the public, and the 500 picturesquely dressed In-Pensioners, are famous tourist attractions; but they are also part of a proudly living military tradition.

More modern, and no less assertive than the Royal Hospital, are the Tate Gallery and the Vickers Building which mark the

way to Westminster. The former, named after its founding benefactor, the sugar-refiner Sir Henry Tate, was erected in 1897; its grandly classical blocks, with their more modern extensions, house one of the nation's greatest collections of painting and sculpture, including notable contemporary works.

From the tall Vickers tower onwards, the scale of the waterfront changes; now we are in the heart of the capital, and passing the headquarters of its political and commercial activity. On the left are the spires and pinnacles of Westminster, on the right the tree-bowered battlements of Lambeth Palace testify to the ancient English alliance of Church and State. Discreetly separated by the width of the Thames from the royal seat of Westminster, Lambeth has been the London residence of the archbishops of Canterbury since the 13th century. Today, in addition, it is the administrative centre of the worldwide Anglican Communion. Among other treasures housed within its walls, the library of some 100,000 volumes is especially important to bibliophiles and historians.

For most visitors, however, the dominant attraction along this reach of the river must be the

Palace and Abbey of Westminster, both of them founded by Edward the Confessor. For five centuries a strongpoint of royal power, the palace is nowadays identified with representative government and parliamentary democracy. The present Houses of Parliament were designed by Sir Charles Barry, following a disastrous fire in 1834, and the buildings, which include the famous Clock Tower housing Big Ben, were completed in 1860 when the Victoria Tower, nearly 400 feet high, was finished. The only major parts of the old royal residence to have survived are the

Continued on page 20

★

ABOVE LEFT: *Chelsea Pensioners in their distinctive scarlet frock coats.*

ABOVE: *A winner of the Watermen's Derby, wearing the Doggett's Coat and Badge. The race was endowed in 1715 by an actor-manager and is rowed on about 1 August from London Bridge to Chelsea.*

FACING PAGE, ABOVE: *Albert Bridge, opened in 1873. The structure is part cantilever, part suspension.*

FACING PAGE, BELOW: *Chelsea houseboats moored near Battersea Bridge.*

FACING PAGE, ABOVE: *The Tate Gallery houses a national collection of British art from the 16th century to about 1900. There are multitudinous oil paintings and watercolours by William Turner, and important works by William Blake and the Pre-Raphaelite School. Alongside are pieces, sometimes highly controversial, by international modern artists.*

FACING PAGE, BELOW: *Lambeth Palace, London seat of the Archbishops of Canterbury, is of great interest. The Lollards Tower is a memorial to John Wycliffe, religious reformer, who was tried here in 1378. The Great Hall was built in the 17th century. In 1787 the first American bishops were consecrated here.*

ABOVE: *The Palace of Westminster, now generally known as the Houses of Parliament, remained a royal residence until Henry VIII moved from here to Whitehall in 1512. The fire of 1834 destroyed everything except Westminster Hall, built in 1097–9 by William II, and Edward III's little Jewel Tower, so the present Houses of Parliament are mid-19th-century. 'Big Ben' in the clock tower was named after Sir Benjamin Hall, Commissioner of Works at that time.*

LEFT: *Lambeth Bridge, with Lambeth Palace visible beyond.*

17

ABOVE: *The architects of the Royal Festival Hall were Robert Matthew and J. Leslie Martin. It was built in 1951 for the Festival of Britain, and has since been hailed as one of the finest concert halls in the world.*

LEFT: *Cleopatra's Needle was presented to Britain in 1819 by Mehemet Ali, Viceroy of Egypt. Whilst it was being towed to England in a watertight case, a storm hit the Bay of Biscay, and the obelisk was abandoned after costing six seamen their lives. Later in the century it was salvaged and was finally brought to London in 1878. Despite the name, it has no connections with Cleopatra.*

FACING PAGE, ABOVE: *County Hall, the headquarters of the Greater London Council, was opened in 1922. The main building was designed by Ralph Knott.*

FACING PAGE, BELOW: *Somerset House became known as the home of the Probate Registry, but recently its Fine Rooms have been restored for exhibitions.*

Great Hall, built by William II between 1097 and 1099, with its magnificent hammer-beam roof dating from the reign of Richard II, and the crypt and cloister of St Stephen's Chapel.

Of the two debating chambers, that of the Lords is much the grander; designed in the most fastidious detail by Augustus Pugin, acting as Barry's assistant, it is considered one of the most brilliant masterpieces of the Gothic Revival, and provides a suitably majestic setting for the great ceremonial occasions of state when Monarch, Lords and Commons are convened in symbolic unity as the Crown-in-Parliament. The House of Commons, by contrast, is relatively austere; Barry designed it so in the first case, and it was rebuilt in even more functional style after its destruction by a German bomb in 1941. Here, however, are enacted some of the principal dramas of English political life; here governments propose laws and defend their records, and here public issues are aired and debated. The reputation of the Mother of Parliaments is perhaps no longer what it was; but Westminster remains a focus for political fascination.

Still more of a national shrine, in every sense, is Westminster Abbey. English kings have been crowned here since the time of William the Conqueror; its vaults

*

ABOVE LEFT: *Southwark Cathedral has Norman remains, as well as an Early English Lady Chapel and an altar screen of 1520 built by Bishop Fox. In the nave is the tomb of John Gower who died in 1408, poet and friend of Chaucer.*

LEFT: *A pleasure launch passes the South Bank complex. The dome of St Paul's Cathedral is visible in the distance.*

FACING PAGE: *St Paul's Cathedral was built by Sir Christopher Wren after the Great Fire, between 1675 and 1710. This floodlit picture shows its magnificent Renaissance exterior, with its great dome.*

are crowded with the tombs and its walls with the memorials of the good, the great and the famous, from saints and poets to generals and politicians; and the countless treasures of art and history which enrich its soaring Gothic beauties make it in all respects a jewel-house of the nation's heritage. Much of the fabric dates from the 14th and 15th centuries, but the western towers, which give the church an outline perhaps as well known as any in Europe, were not added until 1734.

The north bank of the river below Westminster Bridge is closely lined with the massive buildings of central government. For sheer pretentiousness, however, even they cannot rival the gigantically ponderous façade of County Hall, centre of London's local government, or the wind-battered, Orwellian boxes of the Shell Building, both on the south bank. When the tide is low, and mudflats glisten slimily beneath the rattling girders of Charing Cross railway bridge, we see with a vengeance the river's grimly urban aspect, the inspiration of painters such as Monet and Whistler. Here as elsewhere, grey is a tone which seems natural to the south bank, and it is dominant also in the concrete and glass of the clustered 'culture-palaces' which huddle together as if for mutual protection at the south end of Waterloo Bridge. The Royal Festival Hall and National Film Theatre date from 1951; other buildings, including two more concert-halls, an art gallery, and a long-awaited National Theatre, have been added during recent years. They are earnest-looking buildings, but they house music and drama which are the legitimate pride of London.

The north bank, by contrast, speaks here of high Victorian ostentation and endeavour. The broad, leafy boulevard of the Victorian Embankment, created between 1864 and 1870, with its floridly decorated lamps and ponderous stone parapets, runs from Westminster to Blackfriars, past a succession of floating piers and moored vessels which, until recently, included the sturdy little ship HMS *Discovery*, in which Captain Scott of Antarctic fame made his epic voyage from 1900 to 1904. It is now moored in St Katherine's Dock. Among other monuments on the Embankment is the 68 feet high pink granite obelisk from

TOP: *The River Thames from Tower Bridge, with HMS* Belfast *dominating the scene. The gilded flaming urn at the top of the Monument in Fish Street Hill can be clearly seen. The effort of climbing the 311 steps inside the Portland stone column is well rewarded by the splendid view.*

ABOVE LEFT: *During the third week of July, the colourful ceremony of Swan Upping takes place to check and register the Thames swans, which belong partly to the Crown and partly to the Vintners' and Dyers' companies.*

ABOVE RIGHT: *A Billingsgate porter*

wearing the traditional leather hat. The fish market has been moved from the old building, which can be seen below the Monument in the photograph above, to West India Docks.

FACING PAGE: *Southwark Bridge and Cannon Street railway station, taken from the South Bank.*

Heliopolis known as Cleopatra's Needle; dating from *c.* 1500 BC, it was presented to the British people in 1819, but reached its present site only after many adventures.

The area between the river and the Strand was for centuries dominated by great houses and laid out with gardens. York House, Durham House, Arundel House, Essex House and Bridewell Palace are all now no more than names. Somerset House, however, was acquired by the Crown in 1552, and rebuilt by Sir William Chambers between 1776 and 1786; today its coolly elegant façade adds distinction to the riverfront and rebukes the brashness of its neighbours. The 18th century holds sway also in the calm precinct of the Temple, further east, where spacious gardens lap round the rectilinear blocks of lawyers' chambers, austere in detail but imposing in composition, like some measured epitome of the legal ideal.

Beyond Blackfriars we become aware that we have left behind the political, legal, administrative and cultural part of the capital; now the tone is decidedly commercial, even though the ravages of German bombs and the movement of trade downstream have taken much of the life away from the old sea port. But first comes a stretch of river associated with a unique episode in the annals of the theatre, for it was on Bankside, a narrow strip of ground along the south bank where Londoners in Tudor times went to seek their pleasures, that the Elizabethan drama suddenly blossomed and flourished. The site of Shakespeare's Globe Theatre is now a brewery, but the theatrical tradition is carried on by the Mermaid Theatre, opened in 1959, just across the water.

One of the comparatively small number of historic buildings which still survive on the south bank, and one which has close connections with that early heroic period of the English theatre, is Southwark Cathedral, tucked away in a tranquil corner among railway viaducts and roaring lorries. It began its history in the reign of Henry I as the church of an Augustinian priory closely linked to the Bishops of Winchester, who had a palace and much property nearby, including some notorious haunts of evil fame. After the Reformation it became a parish church, and among those buried in its precincts are the Elizabethan dramatists Fletcher and Massinger, and Edmund Shakespeare, brother of the great William, who is himself honoured in a stained-glass window and an alabaster memorial, both of the 20th century. One of the earliest and most distinguished settlers of North America, John Harvard, founder of the university which bears his name, was baptised here in 1607. He is commemorated today in the chapel of St John, specially restored as the Harvard Chapel by members of the university. After narrowly escaping complete demolition on more than one occasion,

and undergoing a series of drastic restorations and rebuildings, the church became a cathedral for the newly-created diocese of Southwark in 1905. Today it is prized as one of the finest Gothic buildings remaining in London.

It needs a considerable effort of the imagination to envisage Elizabethan gallants, ruffed and

*

ABOVE: *Tower Bridge. The Victorian architects who designed its Gothic outlines succeeded in creating an internationally known symbol of London's river.*

LEFT: HMS *Belfast is now a permanent Royal Navy museum. She is moored in the Pool of London.*

FACING PAGE: *The White Tower, founded by William the Conqueror c. 1078. The Traitors' Gate is visible on the left.*

rapiered, swaggering amid the grime of Southwark; but around this stage of our river-voyage the eye is readily caught and the mind stirred by that symbol of a later London, the dome of St Paul's, riding poised yet massive above the rooftops of the City. Sir Christopher Wren's creation no longer presides in unrivalled majesty over a complementary townscape of baroque towers and steeples, as he designed it should in the 1670's; post-war sky-scrapers, even more than Hitler's Blitz, have marred his conception of London's skyline as a harmonious symphony in stone. But the great church still flings its challenge to the clouds.

St Paul's has seen many royal occasions, notably Prince Charles' wedding, but it is much more a national than a royal temple. In times of peril and of triumph, the nation's leaders have joined in solemn prayer at St Paul's. It has watched the rise and fall of empire; its vaults have rung to Marlborough's Te Deums, Nelson is buried here, and Wellington, and at the end of the day the funeral trumpets sounded here beneath the dome for Winston Churchill, last and greatest of imperial statesmen.

Other historic associations than those of imperial grandeur may, however, be evoked by the sight of St Paul's dome. It is for many the characteristic symbol of that almost-vanished City of London, the living town depicted by a series of great writers from Chaucer through Pepys to Dickens. It was a city of winding alleyways and crowded streets, of grand livery halls cheek by jowl with desperate, teeming slums, of galleried inns and dusty ware-houses, of smoke-blackened churches and grimy counting-houses. Above all it was a river-side city, and glimpses of it may still be seen from the river today, lurking at the feet of the wind-whipped office blocks which, like invading aliens, have caused the depopulation of the old town within living memory.

One of the newest things along this reach of the river, in fact, has the oldest name – London Bridge. Here was a principal origin of the City's wealth and importance, marking as it did the upper limit of navigation and the lowest crossing-point before the sea. In fact, until the construction of a bridge at Westminster in the 1740's, it had no rival in the capital. 'Old London Bridge' was built during the last quarter of the 12th century and it carried a street of shops and houses on its 19 narrow arches, much like the Ponte Vecchio which still survives in Florence. It was protected by

two fortified gates and broken by drawbridges, and was graced by a chapel dedicated in honour of the sainted, if debatably saintly, Londoner Thomas Becket. Further edification, of a grisly sort, was offered to passengers in the shape of the mouldering heads of decapitated traitors, which were stuck on poles over the southern gatehouse. This picturesque accumulation survived until 1756, when the buildings were cleared away, but the bridge itself lasted until it was replaced by a classical edifice completed in 1831. Somewhat oddly, this second bridge is now to be found in the vicinity of Lake Havasu City, Arizona, whither it was exported in 1967 in favour of a modern concrete span.

Just by the north end of London Bridge and clearly visible from the river there rises a curious, 202 feet high column, once the monarch of the surrounding streets, though now reduced to insignificance by newer giants. This column, invariably referred to simply as 'the Monument', was completed in 1677 to designs by

Wren, to commemorate the Great Fire of 1666, which was said to have begun in a baker's shop precisely 202 feet away.

Close by on the waterfront is the Victorian building of Billingsgate, where, until 1982, fish were bought and sold for centuries to the accompaniment of a flow of language from the porters so fluently coarse and extravagantly abusive that from the 17th century at least the name of the place has been synonymous with foul speech. The Worshipful Company of Fishmongers, on the other hand, possess their stately livery hall in great dignity some little way upstream, close by the north end of London Bridge.

Downstream again, sobriety is restored by the grey threat of the Royal Navy's last heavy cruiser, HMS *Belfast*, now moored in her retirement off Symon's Wharf. She was the headquarters ship for the Normandy landings from 6 June 1944 onwards and bombarded the coast as commandos went ashore. Those guns may seem puny if we think of modern

missile warfare, but the stacked turrets still carry an aura of power, a hint of naval might past and gone. The year of her launching, 1936, is less than a man's lifetime away, but she seems to ride the stream in ghostly fashion, as if she had survived by accident into an age which no longer understood her.

Vastly more dated, yet somehow also more intimidating, are the fortifications of the ancient royal stronghold which crouches on the north bank opposite HMS *Belfast*. The Tower of London has always been a fortress, an

*

ABOVE: *A Thames sailing barge, with its brown sails unfurled.*

FACING PAGE, ABOVE: *Traditional ships and barges at the Thames Festival.*

FACING PAGE, BELOW: *Designed by Thomas Telford, St Katherine's Dock is now used as a yachting marina and maritime museum. Captain Scott's* Discovery *is also moored here.*

arsenal and a prison rather than a palace in which kings kept court, and its character shows clearly still in its frowning walls and heavily-protected gates. Long after other royal castles have been modified for dignity or comfort, handed away to other uses or simply demolished, the Tower continues patiently in its accustomed role. The Crown

★

FACING PAGE, ABOVE: *The Prospect of Whitby, Wapping, was built during Henry VIII's reign. Samuel Pepys visited this pub many times.*

FACING PAGE, BELOW: *The Port of London Authority's docks are fully modernized to meet the demands of containerization and bulk cargoes.*

ABOVE: *The* Cutty Sark, *launched 1869, was a famous wool clipper.*

Jewels are still kept there, and soldiers are quartered in the barracks; the last State Prisoner was Rudolf Hess, Hitler's Deputy *Führer*; the circuit of the walls is still intact, and the gates are securely locked each night during the age-old ceremony of the Keys.

The central strongpoint of the fortress, and the feature that gives it its name, is the massive Norman keep built for William the Conqueror between *c*. 1078 and 1097, to hold down his newly-acquired City of London. Henry III and Edward I added the outer circuits of walls and towers. As a specimen of medieval military architecture it is fascinating; the collections of arms and armour which it houses – not to mention the regalia displayed in the Jewel House – are priceless; the inhabitants, whether Guardsmen, Yeomen Warders or ravens, are

colourful and picturesque; but in the end it is the fearful tale of imprisonment and torture, murder and execution, which has stained the Tower's stones over the centuries, that draws the visitors and appals the imagination. This is the darker side of our story of royalty, and as the boat slides past Traitors' Gate it is hard to repress a shudder at the thought of those who passed that way in days gone by.

Coupled with the Tower in the tourist's memory is the striking silhouette of Tower Bridge, as much a symbol of London as is the Eiffel Tower of Paris – and even younger, since it dates from 1886 to 1894. Its 1000 ton bascules are lifted comparatively rarely nowadays, for the big ships no longer come to the Pool of London, and the original hydraulic machinery – a marvel of

its time, capable of opening the channel in under two minutes – has recently been replaced by an electrical system.

Until a comparatively short while ago, ships passing downstream through Tower Bridge entered the great complex known as the Port of London, and had to thread their way through a throng of ships and barges which crowded the river and filled the huge dock systems which opened off either bank. But as vessels have grown bigger and transport patterns have changed, the river-trade has moved further downstream – as it has been doing, in fact, for hundreds of years. The medieval quays such as the Queenhythe, mentioned in a charter of Alfred the Great (themselves often incorporating piling from earlier Roman wharfs), lined the north bank above the Tower, and the presence to this day of the Custom House close by Billingsgate Market indicates the position of the old trading centre. In 1696 the first artificial dock, the Great Howland Dock, was built on the south bank at Deptford as a safe anchorage, and later renamed Greenland Dock when used by the whaling fleets, but most shipping continued to crowd on the river throughout the 18th century. A few old inns such as the famous Prospect of Whitby survive as picturesque reminders of this turbulent period. Then in the 19th century a succession of new docks extended the port further and further downstream. St Katharine's Dock close to Tower Bridge is one of the most famous

dating from this period. The Surrey Commercial Docks, the West India and Millwall Docks, the Royal Victoria, the Royal Albert, and further downstream Tilbury Docks – the acreage spread wider and wider – were all controlled from 1909 onwards by the Port of London Authority, who subsequently built the King George V Docks in 1921.

Recent years, however, have seen the most sweeping and rapid changes in all the long history of the port. Those vast inland lakes, so painstakingly created over the last 180 years, have been abandoned in favour of a mighty new development at Tilbury, 25 miles below London Bridge, where the Port of London Authority is shaping one of the biggest container-docks in the world. The ultimate

economic benefits of the move are expected to be great; but the evacuation of old dockland, Stepney, Poplar and Canning Town, has left great social and planning problems, in its wake.

The usual destination of pleasure-voyagers on London's River, however, is not Tilbury but Greenwich, on the south bank five miles downstream from London Bridge. Royal builders were active here from the beginning of the 15th century, and in 1427 Humphrey, Duke of Gloucester, enclosed a park and erected a watchtower on the site later occupied by the Royal Observatory. The original royal palace known as Placentia, or the Pleasaunce, has long since gone, but Henry VIII, Mary I and Elizabeth I were all born there,

and they and their Stuart successors often went there to enjoy the pleasures of a country retreat, while remaining close to the centre of power. Sir Walter Ralegh came too – here at

★

FACING PAGE, ABOVE: *Sir Francis Chichester's* Gipsy Moth IV *in dry dock at Greenwich.* Cutty Sark *in the background.*

FACING PAGE, BELOW: *The National Maritime Museum at Greenwich has many figureheads on show, such as Ajax, the Greek warrior.*

ABOVE: *The Royal Naval College from the river, with the twin domes of the Painted Hall on the right and Chapel on the left.*

Greenwich he is supposed to have laid his cloak across a muddy path before Elizabeth's feet.

But the palmiest days for Greenwich came in the 17th century. In 1616 Inigo Jones was commissioned to build a house for James I's Queen, Anne of Denmark; now known simply as the Queen's House, it is regarded as one of the most important, and perfect, early classical buildings in England. Later in the century, Charles II began to build a palace for himself, which in turn was incorporated after 1694 in Wren's much grander design for a Royal Hospital for seamen, comparable to that established at Chelsea for soldiers. Hawksmoor and Vanbrugh were also associated with the work, which was not fully completed until 1745. The result has been called 'the most stately procession of buildings we possess . . . one of the most sublime sights English architecture affords . . .

where no careless or muddled efforts exist, where, indeed, no mean ideas can live.' In 1873 the Hospital became the Royal Naval College; the Queen's House, much restored, is now part of the National Maritime Museum; and the Old Royal Observatory, also part of the museum, has been returned to its original 17th-century state.

Appropriately, two world-famous sailing vessels, *Cutty Sark* and *Gipsy Moth IV*, lie in drydock nearby.

In contrast to the classical splendours of Greenwich, a short distance down river lies the new Thames Barrier, constructed by the Greater London Council to protect London from the risk of flooding. This magnificent feat of modern engineering, officially opened by the Queen in 1984, dominates the last stretch of the Thames and is a fitting place at which to end our journey down the Royal River.

ABOVE: *The Queen's House, Greenwich.*

★

ACKNOWLEDGMENTS

All pictures are the copyright of Pitkin Pictorials Ltd, with the exception of the following:
Andy Williams: pp iv cover, 1, 13 above, 16/17 below, 22 above; Picturepoint: pp 3 below, 5, 6, 9 above, 12 above; Department of the Environment (Crown copyright, reproduced with the permission of the Controller of Her Majesty's Stationery Office): p 4 above and below; A F Kersting, FIIP, FRPS: 7 above, 8 below, 10 below, 19 above; British Tourist Authority: pp 7 below right, 13 below (Neil Holmes); England Scene: p 7 below left; Kenneth Scowen, FIIP, FRPS: pp 8 above, 10 above left, 11, 15 above, 16 above and below, 18 below, 20 above, 28 above; James Brotherton: p 9 below; Daily Telegraph: pp 10 above right (Charles De Jaeger), 24 below (Michael J Barrett); All Sport: p 12 below; Susan Griggs Agency: pp 14 left, 15 below, 22 below right; Brian Shuel: pp 14 right, 18 above, 22 below left, 27 above and below; Angelo Hornak: pp 16/17 above, 19 below, 21, 32; ZEFA: pp 20 below (Clive Sawyer), 23 (G Mabbs); Richard Hugh Perks: p 26; Port of London Authority (Handford Photography): p 28 below; Spectrum Colour Library: p i cover (Carolyn Clarke). Map, pii cover, by Robert Clark Studios.